To my two sons, KENNETH AND
GLENN, toward whom God has given me
the responsibility of developing them into
mature men in the sight of the Lord and
in the service of men.

Library of Congress Catalog Card Number:
68-31474

Printed in the United States of America

First printing, August 1968
Second printing, November 1968

Devotionals
for modern men

by WILLIAM J. KRUTZA

Baker Book House
Grand Rapids, Michigan 49506

Preface

These meditations are produced in the face of a great paradox. The religion of the Bible from creation to culmination centers in the male gender. God is always referred to as "He." Christ lived among mankind as a man — and a man's man at that.

Scripture portrays Him as the "Son of Man," the "Man of Sorrows," the "Man Christ Jesus."

Church history is replete with great men of faith. Men dominated the leadership of the Early Church, the Church of the Reformation, the Church of the early colonies.

As the centuries passed, the Church, while being dominated by men, has done much for raising the status of women. Using the Bible as its basic sourcebook and building upon its great masculine heritage, you would expect the church still to possess great male appeal. Yet, a survey of an average church reveals that more females than males respond to today's appeal. Beyond this, educational concerns center mostly in children. So when it comes to man's place in church, we apologetically talk about the lack of a

. . . My Father gives you the real heavenly food . . . JOHN 6:33, Berkeley.

men's group or about how difficult it is to appeal to men. We apologize about our lack of thrust toward men.

I trust that I shall motivate Christian men to become manly for Christ. I hope that I shall also appeal to some prospective Christian men who shall flex their muscles and follow Christ. If these things happen, the soul-piercing words of these meditations will have accomplished all I intended.

Before or after a busy day in meat-and-potatoes producing toil, each man needs a few moments to consider what it means to be a man. Each of these meditations, complete in itself, will give you a challenging theme for each day. Each comes straight from the heart and the shoulder — man to man. If you respond as a man you'll become a man among men, following the Biblical pattern.

It is hoped that these meditations might inspire each man to take up his cross daily and follow Christ. Skirted soldiers of Christ will be watching the new recruits.

Contents

*. . . I am the Bread of life. He who comes
to me will never hunger. . .* JOHN 6:35,
Berkeley

SCRIPTURE: And now, from the clay of the ground, the Lord God formed man, breathed into his nostrils the breath of life, and made man a living soul.

— *Genesis 2:7, Knox*

1 And Man Became

The sun, moon, and stars brightened the globe one day in antiquity. Flowering plants graced the earth. Growling animals roamed the fields. Fish of all sorts, sizes, and colors swam unmolested in oceans of water. Yet the earth was incomplete. God's creative genius had yet to reach its pinnacle. Thus in Genesis 1:26 we read, "And God said, Let us create man in our image, after our likeness. . . ."

In the immediacy of the Creator's power "man became." Though God introduced the procreative processes by creating a female, the pinnacle of His work was named *man*. Genesis tells us that that man's name was Adam.

What powers did God entrust to this especially created being? "Man became a living soul." He possessed a distinct feature — a mark not placed within or upon any mineral, animal, or vegetable. Man possessed the ability to reason, to contemplate, to commune with God. This ability was denied all lower creatures — and only God knows why!

God then placed man over all creation to ". . . have dominion over the fish of the sea, and over the fowl of the air, and over the cattle, and over all the earth, and over every creeping thing that creepeth upon the earth" (Genesis 1:26).

Exercising these powers to the fullest extent has never been accomplished by man. That which he was ordained to dominate has often dominated him. Through sin he has revoked his divinely-given primacy. He is totally unable to restore himself to the right relationship to the Creator or even to creation. God, through the redeeming Christ, has provided the only means whereby man can once again realize his potential. Until man encounters this Christ, he will live far below his rightful capacity.

Can you positively state that *you* are realizing your potential? Remember that you are distinguished from all other creatures; therefore as a man you should be demonstrating the reality of the breath of life He has placed in your being. Does your "living soul" function as you answer God's invitation, "Come now, and let us reason together, saith the Lord: though your sins be as scarlet, they shall be as white as snow; though they be red like crimson, they shall be as wool" (Isaiah 1:18)? Does your "living soul" function as you realize the responsibility placed in your hands and heart as God's nature-dominating being?

Are you man enough to accept the position unto which you were created when God "breathed into his [man's] nostrils the breath of life; and he became a living soul?" If you are, you'll find its exalted heights require every ounce of manliness in you to keep yourself at that height — no lower, no higher.

PRAYER: Creator of my soul, help me to dominate everything You put under my authority and still submit to that domination which rightly belongs to You. May I still be as clay in the hand of the One who formed man of the dust of the ground. But once I am made in the new likeness of Christ, keep within me that power that demonstrates that it was God who worked in me both to will and to do His good pleasure. Let the burning breath of the Spirit turn any cowardice in my soul to ashes. Amen.

2 *The Opposite Sex*

The deep significance of God's method of creating a female shocks any attitudes of male supremacy. To make this lovely creature (and an honest human male admits that the female is more beautiful to behold than the male, whereas in lower creatures the situation is almost universally reversed) God anesthetized the man Adam by sleep. God removed a rib, and with a touch of delicate chest surgery "closed up the flesh" and produced Woman. The creative act in bringing forth "the mother of all living" (Genesis 3:20) remains no less spectacular than the creation of the male in the first place.

Contemplate the significance of taking the rib. The Jamieson, Fausset, and Brown Commentary states, "She was not made out of the head to surpass him, nor from his feet to be trampled on, but from his side to be equal to him, and near his heart to be dear to him." Matthew Henry adds, ". . . under his arm to be protected, and near his heart to be beloved."

It's not unusual that we've developed the term "the opposite sex." Surely, it's true in more than a biological sense. The psychological makeup of a woman differs greatly from that of the man. The emotions of tenderness, sympathy, and affection seem to be inborn in a woman. Not so with man. Naturally he'd tend to be gruff and unaffectionate. When we say "she is a woman's woman" we mean something as far removed as

China is from Chicago as to say "he is a man's man." We boast about a he-man but never refer to a she-woman! We expect women to have specific character traits. We expect men to have different traits. Both perform specific psychological functions in life.

Likewise, every man has specific duties to perform. So does every woman. The fact that Eve was dependent upon Adam, or should we rather say that God's chosen method of creating woman depended partly upon His former creation of man, doesn't allow man the privilege of superiority. In duties, man is placed in authority, but in spirit and in flesh he can claim no superior position. In his union with Eve we find no "I-am-above-you" attitude suggested by Adam. He was thrilled to have her around.

How close to your heart has God placed one of the opposite sex? Is there a cleaving or a cleavage between you? How dear has she become, especially if you've been granted the Divinely-allowed one-flesh privilege described in Genesis 2:24?

It takes genuine manliness to accept God's positioning of women. The opposite sex can't be trampled on — she was not produced from the heel — but from the rib, from beneath man's heart. One wonders if the glory God has placed upon her through the privilege of bringing forth children might sometimes outshine the glories man acclaims to himself. Be man enough to respect the female's role in life. In thus doing, you'll enhance your own.

PRAYER: Lord, I stand amazed when contemplating that You created another's body even more complex than mine. I vow to cherish, comfort, and sustain the helpmeet that You, in consideration of my need, have sent my way. Amen.

SCRIPTURE: And the man said, The woman whom thou gavest to be with me, she gave me of the tree, and I did eat. — *Genesis 3:12, ASV*

3 Blame Your Wife

No time lapses in Eden's beautiful garden have been recorded. It seems unlikely that Adam had time enough to forget how Eve arrived on the scene. Nor could he have forgotten the eulogy he had uttered in her behalf, God being his chief witness.

The tragedy of Eden cannot all be recorded on the serpent's ledger. Nor would any manly individual pull the Adam trick — or would he? Which one of us would have wanted to have been in his boots — I mean skin?

To avoid the moral responsibility for his act of disobedience whereby he partook of the forbidden fruit, Adam pointed his bony finger toward heaven and toward the woman.

"The woman whom *thou* gavest to be with me." Since God created Eve, surely God must be partially at fault when she did wrong. In the same fashion as an automobile owner accuses the Detroit designer when something misfires in the engine, so Adam pointed an accusing finger toward the Divine Designer. "There must have been something wrong when You put the model together in the first place!"

Secondly, Adam accused his wife. "*She* gave me of the tree." A cowardly innocence to say the least. The man blamed his wife for his misdeeds. How much like the sister-brother arguments that happen in almost every home during growing-up days — "She did it!" Seemingly the first one to make the accusation feels his conscience is cleared, even though he might be as guilty as the accused.

The cowardice produced by sinning always looks for a scapegoat. For Adam it was his wife. For you it might be the same. Blame your wife's cooking when you come home grouchy after a disagreement at the office. Blame your wife's hosting when you fail to clench a business deal. Blame your wife's planning when you come home late and have to rush to an appointment she made for you during the day. Since your masculine voice has more resonance, let her take the full blast of your accusations as soon as you get inside the door. Follow Adam if you want to be like him. Whenever something goes wrong, or whenever you do something wrong, your wife is the easiest to blame.

If Adam were a genuine man, he'd have emphasized "and *I* did eat." But we almost miss this phrase when we give it the typical manish reading. It takes mature character to say, "I did wrong; I have sinned; it's my fault." But somehow it gets things running clockwise; it sets the sails of your marriage vessel into the full gusts of God's blessing power; it gets others to respect you as a real man!

Shouldering the full responsibility for your own behavior, your own spiritual development, your own mental acumen, your own advancement or failure, makes you a man. And besides, when you come face to face with God, you can't blame your wife anyway!

PRAYER: All-seeing and all-knowing God, You see through all the cover-up I make for my failings and sins. Forgive me for blaming others, especially the one dearest to me. Give me the moral courage to stand or fall on my own accomplishments. Help me to rely fully upon the righteousness which is to be had in Christ. Amen.

SCRIPTURE: By faith Abraham, on being called, obeyed in starting off for a country which he was to receive as his own, and he did it in spite of the fact that he did not know where he was going.

— *Hebrews 11:8, Williams*

4 When Security Doesn't Matter

On occasions God shatters man's well-established retirement benefit plans by placement in new positions, some of which do not guarantee after-65 ease.

To be sure, Abraham had social security at Ur. His stock was numbered by the hoof, and he was little concerned about any Dow-Jones averages. His stock was always good. But security was something he enjoyed both at Ur and at Haran. He could have enjoyed an upper middle-class type life at either location for a long time — even till death brought him into the position of ultimate security — eternal security!

But the Lord definitely had another plan. In Genesis 12:1, He instructed Abraham (Abram), "Get thee out of thy country, and from thy kindred, and from thy father's house, unto a land that I will show thee."

In Hebrews 11:8 we notice Abraham's maturity. It's wrapped up in one word — "obeyed." Security no longer mattered because Abraham obeyed his God. Obedience became the greatest security he could have. A personal grasp of God's command made a new man out of him — he became a man of faith. Security with God even in the unseen became the stabilizing, energizing force in his life.

At the focal point of obedience, God met Abraham with His eternal resources. When Abraham obeyed even to the point of not knowing what security he'd ever have in the new land, he found his new security in God himself.

The security of the seen, the temporal, the lifetime of thrift and wise business practice is no match for the security of doing God's bidding. History reveals sad stories of men and empires that placed life's highest values in amassing capital gains. Their money often dissipated overnight. The security of military force vanished on blood-soaked battlefields. Still men proudly hold onto their riches as the ultimate in life.

Don't we have the total right to our possessions? Aren't we entitled to the enjoyment of the fruits of our labors? Have we not amassed all this for our retirement? Don't we deserve to collect all we've paid in — and more? From the seen viewpoint — yes. But you must face God. Is he saying to you, "Get thee out . . . unto . . . that I will show thee?" If He is, all your securities don't really matter — only He remains.

Can you afford to select temporal earthly security instead of an eternally designed plan? Do you have the faith to go forth even unto an unknown destination, into unventured territory, doing new things? If so, you qualify for the reward of obedience. God shall be your security — and in the end might allow you more blessed earthly security than you possessed at the first. But, like Abraham, security can't matter now; obedience is the only criteria. Are you man enough to obey God?

PRAYER: Lord, I've read about faith. I know what the Bible says about it. Somehow I've lacked the adventuresomeness and courage to translate my faith into obedience. Help me to take my moving orders from You and trust the results of my obedience to Your wisdom. For Christ's sake, Amen.

5 The Grace to Give Others the Best

No sooner had Abraham come to the northern part of the land God was going to show him, than he had another blow to his security. The servants of his nephew Lot began to argue with his servants. Seemingly there wasn't grazing area or water sufficient for the huge flocks of both men. Abraham was put to a new test. Would his character show signs of maturity displayed in his home-transplanting answer to God's previous call?

Stretched out before Abraham and Lot were the green plains of the Jordan valley. These could easily supply food and water for all of their flocks, plus many more. Could this be the "land that I will show thee" promised in Genesis 12:1? The fulfillment of God's promise seemed so easy, almost too simplified. Now it was challenged — not by someone greater than Abraham, but by someone lesser than he. To give in to Lot appears to be a defeat for faithful Abraham. Yet Abraham makes the proposal: "Choose the section you want; I'll take what is left; I'll go the other direction."

You've probably worked hard for everything you've attained or amassed to this point in life. Success seems only one step

16

beyond the mountain peak which is set before you. But wait, someone else is on that peak beside you — a younger man. He's merciless in pushing himself to the top. He really doesn't deserve the plush. But the challenge faces you. One of you will get the gravy. One of you will reach the summit. Do you possess the Christian grace to give him the best choice? Would you be satisfied to eke out your living at the present level?

The Christian man often faces the challenge of allowing others to make choices either to the Christian's benefit or reversal. What type of decision would you make under similar circumstances? Would you be able to demonstrate the bigness of heart evidenced in Abraham? Could you gracefully allow someone to take the best, or to take his pick of what was available?

Young Lot seized the opportunity and headed toward the green valley. Abraham was left to go to the barren, rolling hills of Canaan. He possessed the manly maturity that allowed someone else to leap forward to success. Because of this grace to give the good grazing land to Lot, God recorded Abraham's name among the faithful. Not that Abraham sought such a registry, for it was made many centuries after his death, but that he attained it as a tribute to his character.

Possession of this grace is a noble accomplishment. Few men attain it. Sorry to say, few Christians possess the ability and grace to say, "I'll take what's left." Are you numbered among the few or are you just another member of the crowd?

PRAYER: Lord Jesus, You suffered the loss of all things for my eternal benefit. Make me willing to suffer temporal setbacks if it will show what You are like. Amen.

SCRIPTURE: Abraham dwelt in the land of Canaan, and Lot dwelt in the cities of the Plain, and moved his tent as far as Sodom. Now the men of Sodom were wicked and sinners against Jehovah exceedingly.

— *Genesis 13:12, 13, ASV*

6 *Problems of the Plush*

Abraham didn't get such a bad deal after all. He at least could breathe the clear air that softly blew across the Canaanite hills. With clear conscience, he could gaze at the Milky Way or at the evening stars. Grubbing for his sheep and cattle kept him and his servants occupied physically and faithful spiritually. Only God could make his cattle and sheep prosper on those arid wastelands.

Lucky Lot didn't have to bother looking for green patches of grass or cool springs of water. These were everywhere in abundance. He had plenty of leisure time in which to pursue his own interests and amusements. Why not let his tent in close proximity to the entertainment centers of Sodom and Gomorrah?

But Lot soon encountered some of the problems of the plush. These weren't income tax problems either; they were moral problems. They were concerned with the very purposes of life. They challenged Lot's religion.

When a man makes "being well-fixed" his goal, he'll soon come face to face with other problems beyond those created by an internal revenue officer. Keeping good account of assets and liabilities is no difficult problem with a little bookkeeping skill, but keeping account of the moral and spiritual values of the plush life becomes quite taxing.

If suddenly you've "come into the bucks" either by inheritance or wise business practices or retirement, you will face the challenges Lot had. Up to this time you realized to some extent the meaning of your stewardship of time, talent, and treasures. Now you can purchase the things you missed during working days. Now you can afford an extra vacation. Now you can afford those items you previously considered luxuries. Beware, the bright lights of Sodom and Gomorrah that beamed into Lot's open tent door have as much power to blind the soul as the direct light of an eclipsed sun has power to blind the eyes.

The real man stood in the Canaanite hills having communion with God, being satisfied with lesser things. And in due course, God called him forth to rescue his plushly endowed nephew.

The real problems of the plush center in its ability to satisfy man's soul. Lot pitched his tent toward Sodom. Soon he "dwelt in Sodom" (Genesis 14:12). Later on "Lot sat in the gate of Sodom" (Genesis 19:1) as a judge, a politician, a ruler of the city council. The very plush that attracted Lot to Sodom soon enslaved him.

To seek wealth for itself and the entertainment it can buy is to court inner decay and eventual destruction. If the plush life comes to you, learn that it simply remains as a trust of which you are the executor accountable to God. If need be, pitch the tent of your life toward the barrenness and poverty of the world to maintain the Christian view of earthly gains.

PRAYER: God, I admit the inner longing to accomplish some cherished dreams. If You will entrust me with the means to accomplish any dreams, first purify these inner longings; then help me to accomplish what You desire. Amen.

SCRIPTURE: Jabez appealed to the God of Israel, saying, "Wilt Thou grant me a true blessing and extend my boundaries; let Thy hand be with me, and keep calamity from me so that no pain assails me," and God brought about what he had requested.

— *I Chronicles 4:10, Berkeley*

7 A Praying Man, That's All!

Praying men are not a rarity in the Bible. Recall the thunderous prayer of Elijah on Mt. Carmel or the polished dedicatory prayer of Solomon before the Temple. Visualize the king-defying Daniel on his knees three times a day before an open window, praying to the living God. Recall Christ in Gethsemane or Peter's cry on Galilee's choppy waters. Or pick the classic example of how not to pray given by Jesus in the illustration of the Pharisee who went up to the Temple and prayed with himself. After such a review, why should we pick out a character who is mentioned in only two verses of the entire Bible and label him a praying man?

What makes the record of Jabez stand above his peers is the fact that he prayed. We know nothing else about him. We know that his mother gave him his name because she "bare him with sorrow." We are not even enlightened as to the type or extent of her sorrow.

In clear-cut pleas he requests God to favor him by enlarging his coasts — either in the enlargment of earthly goods or spiritual influence, and that the hand of the Lord would be with him — that he'd know the personal guidance of God (perhaps to outsmart some enemy), and that God would keep him from evil, that it would not grieve or dominate him. To these simple requests came God-given answers. "God granted him that which he requested."

20

Jabez was a special kind of man among the long lists of genealogies in the Biblical record. The distinction of being able to pray was his only distinction. Being known as a praying man and being able to get specific answers to prayer seemed to remain out of the grasp of most of his contemporaries. At least, no mention of their prayer fetes are recorded for future generations to observe. Not so with Jabez — all men remember him as a man of prayer.

A man of prayer — this isn't the designation given to a person who can't do other things. Too often manly fellows equate praying about life's great problems with indecision and cowardice. This can be the case with some men, but not with Jabez. Some people say, "Let's pray about it," when they ought to get off their knees and "do something about it." Others whose lives have been saturated with a false piety seem to feed their spirituality by putting items on their prayer lists.

But let's not make the collossal mistake of saying no men with backbone pray. Look at Christ, Daniel, the Apostle Paul. How about Abraham Lincoln or General Douglas MacArthur or astronaut John Glenn or Senator Mark Hatfield? To be known as a praying man isn't the designation for a mental, moral, or spiritual pigmy. It is the designation of a spiritual giant. The man who can pray will always be head and shoulders above those around him. Does God see you above the crowd? Will the annals of the future record your name as one who talked his daily affairs and desires over with the Creator?

PRAYER: Lord, the language I use in conversation with You seems so clumsily stated. Maybe it's because I don't talk often enough with You. Forgive and cleanse me from depending upon myself when all along I should commit the concerns of my life to You. Also, while I'm thinking about it, enlarge my concerns for others. Teach me to persevere in conversation with You. Amen.

SCRIPTURE: In the year that king Uzziah died I saw the Lord . . . Then said I, Woe is me! for I am undone; because I am a man of unclean lips.

— *Isaiah 6:1, 5, ASV*

8 A Man Sees Himself

Go to a mirror and take a good look at yourself. Next, go to your desk and write a description of what you saw in the mirror. Let someone read your description for accuracy!

Isaiah came face to face with the mirrored image of himself when the brightness of the presence of the Lord shone into his life. An amazing scene is pictured for us. Ushered into the presence of the Lord, he beheld the shining glory of the Almighty. He understood something of the holiness of Jehovah. He said, "I saw [I understood or I comprehended] the Lord." This can be added to the physical interpretation of the text without any injustice being done. Surely there was some physical manifestation with the Temple being filled with smoke, but there was much more!

A coward would run. A hypocrite would excuse himself. A theologian would explain. But manly Isaiah did none of these. The gaze at God only revealed to him the nature of his inward personality. And what he saw shocked him. When he had an opportunity to sketch what was reflected in the mirror of God's call and presence, he could only cry out concerning the desperate condition of his soul, "Woe is me! for I am undone."

Anyone checking Isaiah's description of himself might seek to pacify him with, "You're not as bad as you say you are." He'd retort that he had seen God in glorious purity and holiness. How else could he view himself?

Look again at Isaiah's description of himself. " 'Woe is me!

for I am undone.' Undone — unworthy, unclean, utterly sinful, helpless to do anything about it. 'For I am a man of unclean lips.' My lips only voice what is harbored in my soul. Out of the heart the mouth speaks — and my tongue tells the tale of my heart — unclean.

"Besides this, 'I dwell in the midst of a people of unclean lips.' " This might give some coward a little feeling of relief around Isaiah, because he saw everyone else just as evil as he. Possibly Isaiah could have thought, "I'm not so bad. Look at everyone else for awhile!" But that isn't the meaning Isaiah gave to the situation. What he really meant was, "I am no better than anyone else; my heart and lips are as unclean as theirs."

You are a man. But are you man enough to stand in the revealing presence of God and see yourself as you really are? Can you take the ego-crashing scene? Can you stand the pride-shattering presence of the revelation of your personal spiritual state? Dare you become a man who sees himself as he really is?

If you can stand the soul-searching pressure, stand in the presence of God with your soul exposed to the brightness of His person. Cry out in the words of Isaiah, which will reveal your readiness to go under the searching, revealing work of the Holy Spirit and your readiness to go up to higher planes of spiritual maturity. It takes a real man to see himself as God views all men. It takes a real man to respond in the attitude of Isaiah. Are you a man?

PRAYER: In the reflective power of Your majestic Person, I cringe to view myself. Implant godly courage in my soul — spiritual starch in my spine, so I'll be able to face You and myself. Then when I utter Isaiah's wail, bring the forces of the cleansing of the blood of Christ into action in my life so something is done to my whole personality. Amen.

SCRIPTURE: Then the Lord said to Cain, Where is thy brother Abel! I cannot tell, said he; is it for me to keep watch over my brother? — *Genesis 4:9, Knox*

9 A Man and His Brother

Throughout the Bible, God seems to show a genius for asking probing and sometimes embarrassing questions. Jesus asked His disciples, "Whom do ye say that I am?" Questions of divine origin continually penetrate the souls of men. God never asks superficial questions just to pass the time of day.

In this encounter, God had previously asked Cain three questions: "Why art thou wroth? Why is thy countenance fallen? If thou doest well, shalt thou not be accepted?" (Genesis 4:6, 7).

Now comes the question to test the full manhood of Cain, "Where is Abel thy brother?" God did not ask it because He didn't know Abel's whereabouts. The all-knowing God, who knows the timetables of the motions of millions of stars, surely could keep track of the slow movements of one of His earth creatures. Abel's soul had already slipped into the presence of its Creator. In His omniscience, God could have recited the total theological explanation of what happens to a man's soul when a man dies. But He chose not to do this.

Relating properly to other men, regardless of blood relationships, is one of the greatest tests of man's moral character. Cain flunked the test. He took the easy way out — he lied, "I know not." He knew that Abel's body was in the exact position it fell when he murdered him. He probably spent considerable time viewing what happened to Abel, since he hadn't seen any other man die previous to this. He probably knew the angle of Abel's fall. Possibly he had even covered the body with leaves, fearing his act would be discovered by man or beast. But in his lying to God, he presented a problem that forced the question he asked to have only one answer.

How could God answer him negatively? "Am I my brother's keeper?" Who else could be?

As a man, would you resort to lying in such a vital matter? Are you man enough to positively answer Cain's question? Am I my brother's keeper when it comes to someone whose skin pigment is different than mine? Am I my brother's keeper when it comes to the underprivileged of the world? Am I my brother's keeper when his political or religious philosophy doesn't mesh with mine? Or am I my brother's keeper simply when my brother agrees with me? Am I my brother's keeper only when he and I enjoy equal or nearly equal social status?

The consequences of a positive answer to Cain's question will lead anyone to a new view of the stewardship of life, a new view of race relations, a new view of charity. Are you equipped to face the consequences of the Christian answer to this burning social and moral question that spans the centuries and calls for present application? You might have to give more of your money to missions if you answer it properly. You might have to forsake the race prejudices you've cherished in the past. You might have to show a new compassion to the world's needy — even to those in a nearby big city slum. You might have to rethink any bigoted philosophies you have held and propagated.

Cain wasn't a man any longer. His manliness disappeared in the crucial hour, if perchance he had any previous to this encounter with God. This question has a way of separating the men from the boys. Yes, you are your brother's keeper. Act accordingly.

PRAYER: Since You stick closer than a brother, help me to see my responsibilities to all men. Help me not to rationalize theologically when others are in desperate need. Help me to follow Christ's pattern by doing good even unto the least of men. Thus I shall do it unto You. Amen.

SCRIPTURE: Obadiah revered the Lord so much that
when Jezebel cut down the prophets of the Lord, Obadiah took a hundred prophets and hid them by fifties
in a cave and provided them with bread and water.
— I Kings 18:3, 4, Berkeley

10   Being A Hidden Disciple

Before you condemn Obadiah or the hundred prophets for
cowardice, check to see if you have ever faced a formidable
enemy of Jezebel's calibre!

Jezebel was fearless in her wickedness. She determined to
crush anyone who would oppose her lustful desires. Even the
outspoken, thundering prophet Elijah ran from her because she
vowed to add him to her list of ex-prophets.

Obadiah was governor of Ahab's house. He was a God-fear-
ing Israelite in a place of responsibility and reputation. Other
Israelites probably knew of his consecration to God and
respected him for it much like we respect and admire born-
again Christians in responsible governmental positions in our
nation today.

Obadiah was a sort of Central Intelligence Agency man in
Ahab's court. He had first-hand intelligence information concerning Jezebel's planned anti-religious activities. He was
able to thwart her scheme by hiding the prophets fifty at a
time in a cave. From his position he tapped the government
supply house to procure food for the prophets. Thus he successfully circumvented the wrath of the wicked queen and
probably wasn't detected in his counter-Jezebel tactics. He
seemed well-hidden in the governmental structure.

Before you completely vindicate Obadiah and the prophets,
ask yourself a soul-stunning question: Can one remain a hidden
disciple of the Lord? Does this conflict with the true prophet's
position and message from the Lord, both in the Old Testament
and in the New Testament? Is a prophet a prophet when he

is silent? Is it cowardice to remain silent in the face of gross wickedness?

In contrast to Obadiah's approach to life as a prophet, we read the piercing words of Christ, "Ye are the light of the world. A city that is set on a hill cannot be hid. Neither do men light a candle, and put it under a bushel, but on a candlestick; and it giveth light unto all that are in the house" (Matthew 5:14, 15). The light that has shined into a believer's heart must radiate. Even the Old Testament, if believed and practiced, urged the Israelites to win others to the faith.

To hide our witness is a travesty against the New Testament. The Gospel demands that each of us goes and tells the message.

A prophet is not a prophet when he is silent. He misses his calling by not proclaiming the message God has demanded that he proclaim. He must be a forthteller as well as a foreteller. Woe be to that prophet who becomes tongue-tied, who worries about his own skin more than about God's attitude toward wickedness.

Only a coward remains silent in the face of wickedness. Who shall rebuke and rebuff wickedness unless it is we who believe in righteousness? And we must do this at the opportune time, in the opportune place, and in the right manner.

Of course, the value of letting your life prove the value of the message of your lips cannot be underestimated. But be honest, how much living must be done to back up the few statements of faith most of us utter? Amidst the wickedness of our era, God is speaking to us to be in places where righteousness challenges men to change their ways of life. He is seeking vocal prophets who dare oppose the downward trends. Be a man — come out of hiding.

PRAYER: Spirit of God, enable me to back up Christian deeds with Christian words. Let me have less fear to oppose wickedness and to warn the wicked of the judgments of God. I'll take the bushel basket off my witness. Amen.

SCRIPTURE: And Ahab said to Obadiah, "Come let us go about the land and look for all the springs and all the brooks; perhaps we may find pasture to keep alive horses and mules and not be deprived of the cattle."

— *I Kings 18:5, Berkeley*

11 When Mules Were More Valuable than Men

The thunderous prayer of Elijah had shut up the clouds. For more than three years it hadn't rained. By this time, Palestinian deserts were powder piles of wind-blown dust. Finding green grass was like finding the proverbial needle in a barnyard fodder pile. No wonder King Ahab and Queen Jezebel weren't fond of Elijah the Tishbite. By now almost all the inhabitants of the land were clamoring for the king to invent some type of salt-free mass irrigation system.

But the thwarted, self-centered, self-indulgent minds of the king and queen blocked out their concern for people. The king went to his house governor, Obadiah, with one request, "Find grass and water for the horses and mules." That was the most important consideration at the time!

"So they divided the land between them to pass throughout it: Ahab went one way by himself, and Obadiah went another way by himself" (I Kings 18:6). We have already questioned the moral maturity of Obadiah. Now, under the orders of a godless king he shows himself again as spineless. Together they lost their sense of values — mules became of greater value than men!

Concern for selfish gains always leads one to place personal possessions and the means of gaining a sought-for end above the moral values involved. Obadiah for one, if he had even the least corpuscle of starch in his vertebrae, would probably have questioned the fulfillment of Ahab's desires for mules instead of men. He became so engrossed in the king's business that he could easily shove moral considerations into some secondary dark corner of his mind.

You might not go as far in pursuit of selfish ends as did Ahab, but what inner guarantees do you have that you aren't pursuing self-centered interests? Do you have the courage to rise above the moral decay around you? Or are you so involved in the things you are doing to please those for whom you work that you willingly compromise your moral standings or reject involvement in the work of your church?

Too often men get so busy that they refuse to take leadership positions in the church. They say they wouldn't have time to attend all the committee meetings, that such meetings might interfere with their bowling night or the investment club meeting.

Are Christian men much better off in God's sight than was Ahab (except for his willful wickedness in worshiping pagan deities) if they are self-seeking? Dr. A. W. Tozer lists the ridding of one's life of self-seeking as one major step to the holy life. According to this standard, are you holy or unholy in God's sight? Do your possessions mean more to you than the souls of men? Are your stocks (compared to Ahab's mules) of greater concern to you than the needs of thirsty, starving humanity?

PRAYER: Lord, it's easy to become self-seeking because even self-preservation requires a certain amount of expended energy. And when the comforts of my family are involved, I put extra effort into my work so I can provide what they desire. I confess that in this, I sometimes lose sight of the important moral considerations of life — and lose interest in the souls of miserable people around me. Help me to maintain the sensitivity that Christ displayed toward others in need. Amen.

SCRIPTURE: After this, Moses and Aaron obtained audience with Pharaoh, and said to him, We have a message to thee from the Lord God of Israel, Give my people leave to go and offer me the sacrifice in the desert. — *Exodus 5:1, Knox*

12   When to Face the Ungodly

A certain Christian, a used-car dealer, always boasted that he testified to every person from whom he purchased a car or to the customer to whom he sold a car. Usually this witness was of the bulldozer style. He'd begin talking about his honesty in business and then clobber his hearer with the reasons for his honesty — his Christian experience. From this he launched into an evangelistic approach that made the hearer look quite ridiculous if he or she refused the salesman's invitation to respond immediately to Jesus Christ. People usually thought he was some type of religious kook and were glad to see him leave.

Lest some man tries to make a self-comforting position for not testifying, let him read the sad story of prophet Obadiah's life in Ahab's court. Because all situations don't lend themselves to preaching a sermon doesn't mean that no situations lend themselves to a pungent personal testimony.

Facing ungodly men takes considerable preparation. And unfortunately too many church men are poorly prepared. Are you of this variety? If so, note the preparation Moses made before facing ungodly Pharaoh. He didn't rush into the presence of this highminded, cultured Egyptian unprepared. Don't miss the significance of the first two words of the text above, "After this." This lets us in on something that happened beforehand.

Moses had several hurdles to leap. The first one was hurdled at the burning bush. He realized there that God had put in a call for his life — something that is essential in every man's life if he's to be a man among men.

God proclaimed, "I AM THAT I AM . . . Thus shalt thou say unto the children of Israel, I AM sent me unto you" (Exodus 3:14). That settled it: Moses went forth because God called him. Do you have the assurance of such a call, such a claim upon your life? You need it if you are ever going to effectively face the ungodly!

Next Moses had the beforehand preparation of the words, "And thou shalt say unto Pharaoh, Thus saith the Lord" (Exodus 4:22). A personal encounter with God equipped him to know what he was going to say. The words he spoke were those of God demanding that Pharaoh do something for the captive Israelite slaves. Moses thundered the words of a thundering God, "Thus saith the Lord God of Israel."

How is your book learning? Do you know enough Scripture to face ungodly men, not with philosophical arguments, but with the Word of the living God? Against the powerful "Thus saith the Lord" there can be little effective argument. Sure, Pharaoh rebelled, but his rebellion was costly. In the end he recognized God's Word as truth and God's way as sovereign!

As a man among ungodly men, you'll be prepared to face them if you get pre-preparation. "Study to show thyself approved unto God, a workman that needeth not to be ashamed . . ." (II Timothy 2:15).

PRAYER: Lord, save me from facing a formidable foe until I prepare my soul for the battle. Give me a sponge-like ability to fill myself with Your Word. Reinforce my soul with the assurance of Your call. To glorify Christ, Amen.

13 Just One Shady Business Deal

The community of goods idea of Acts 4:32-37 seemed like a workable plan for the early church. People of means, in selling their vested interests, were able to equalize the income and prestige of even the economically poorest Christians. They sold their possessions, laid the money at the apostles' feet, and expected nothing more than an equally proportionate share. This practice was not obligatory. Each chose to do as he pleased. But once the choice was made, the Holy Spirit verified it to the apostles.

Ananias was a wise investor previous to his conversion. He had saved enough money to invest in some private property. The type of property indicated by the word "possession" was a piece of real estate, "the land" (Acts 5:8). Being a landowner, he probably had accumulated more than average wealth. Thus, when he sold it and gave part of the money to the apostles, his gift was probably a sizeable one.

To sell property for profit produces no sin — except that that profit be exorbitant. An exorbitant profit indicates an attempt to take advantage of the buyer. There's no indication Ananias thus sinned.

The shadiness of his only business deal was in his lying about the profit. He deliberately tried to make the church sympathetic with his accepted relative poverty so he could collect the equalized share being distributed and yet feast upon the receipts of his personal sale. The Holy Spirit detected his shady self-benefiting dealing.

If the keenness displayed by the Spirit-empowered apostles was evidenced today, how many men of the church would stand as red-faced as Ananias and his wife? The greed for gold causes many to cheat God, themselves, and others. Yet they pride themselves in being good givers.

Business deals are not simply on the human level for the Christian. A vertical dimension always enters every business transaction. Had Ananias known God was going to expose his shady deal, he'd probably have come clear in the first place. Probably Sapphira his wife would have told the truth if she knew of God's wrath upon her husband.

Because God doesn't seem to move in such decisiveness in punishing sin today, many Christian men adopt the "get all the profit you can" practices of ungodly men. They often attempt to appear poor to attract the sympathy of others. True Christianity demands that men be honest in all business dealings. It also requires honesty in the reporting of the same. Can your financial statement stand the scrutinizing eye of the Holy Spirit. Or would you be as dead as Ananias and his wife if God chose to deal with you like He dealt with them? Shadiness in even one small business deal cannot command the approval of God — even if you gave the total profit to His work!

PRAYER: Omniscient God, be the auditor of all my business transactions. Keep me honest to the n'th degree so my business contacts will testify of Your daily control of my life. In the name of Him whose very being is integrity. Amen.

SCRIPTURE: I appeal to you for my child Onesimus
. . . For perhaps it was for this reason that he was
parted from you for awhile, that you might have him
back forever, not as a slave any longer but more than
a slave, a dearly loved brother.

— *Philemon 10, 15, 16, Williams*

14   When an Employee Bypasses the Boss

If you're the boss, a foreman, or the head of a department, you've probably had one of your employees bypass you with a suggestion for improvement of some company operation. Maybe he bypassed you with a complaint. Your reaction to the knowledge of his actions indicated the development (or lack of development) of your Christian character and manliness.

The situation described in Paul's letter to Philemon isn't much different. Onesimus was the employee of Philemon. He bypassed (ran away from) his owner (boss). He appealed his case to one (Paul) who exerted influence upon his boss. Paul, the boss' superior, gave instruction that Onesimus return to his position. But, get this, he also instructed boss Philemon how he was to react toward this employee after the return.

Wow! You say all that's in a little letter near the end of the New Testament? It's there if you're man enough to apply it. It's a masterpiece in employer-employee relations.

When you (a person who has some authority over others) are bypassed by an employee, you can react in several ways.

Some bosses have the "I'll show him" attitude. From then on, they scrutinize each employee's work with special care. They see to it that the boss-challenging employee isn't given much authority. They even shift the work so such an employee must continually depend upon the boss. Some bosses begin to minimize the Onesimus-type employee's skills, thus providing an excuse to terminate his or her employment.

If you have the Christian manliness and maturity that Paul expected to find in Philemon, you will profit from the employee's bypass and willingly accept the advice given even by one below you. Philemon accepted Onesimus as a brother even though the employment status remained the same — Onesimus remained a slave! And Paul, Philemon's superior, stated this was the only possible Christian way of acceptance. Through Onesimus' bypass and Philemon's new acceptance, the character of Philemon showed itself to be genuinely transformed by Jesus Christ.

How greatly we need this grace today — even in Christian missionary organizations, denominational headquarters, publishing houses, and other businesses operated by Christians. The ability to accept those who bypass us in seeking to present their ideas is a Christian trait difficult to develop or practice. Could you show this Christian ability if an Onesimus presented himself in your place of employment today?

PRAYER: Enlarge my heart, O God, to allow those who work with or for me to express themselves. Then allow me the grace to accept their suggestions or criticisms without depreciating their position or importance. Help me to do this in the name of the One who humbled Himself and now makes me a co-laborer with Himself. So shall we work together as Christian brothers to honor our Master. Amen.

SCRIPTURE: Hearing that, Pilate asked if the man were a Galilean and, ascertaining that He came under Herod's jurisdiction, he remitted Him to Herod, who was himself in Jerusalem during those days.

— *Luke 23:6, 7, Berkeley*

15 *Passing the Buck*

The responsibility for the death of Jesus Christ had to be pinned on someone. And Pilate didn't want the label. He responded like most humans when responsibility for a misdeed has to be attached to some person. He sought for a quick way out.

What made Pilate so fidgety? Was it because in cross examination of the criminal, he found Jesus free from all guilt? Did he not exclaim, "I find no fault in this man" (Luke 23:4)? Did he have an inkling of a conscience? a thread-thin respect for justice? He probably did, but he lacked the manly courage to support convictions with deeds. Rather, in this pressure-filled case, he sought to "pass the buck."

The word "Galilee" came in full stereophonic sound to his ears. It sounded better than the word "water" sounds to a thirsty Sahara Desert traveler. Galilee was out of his domain. He could push Christ onto Herod. Then he could laugh up his sleeve as he heard how Herod squirmed under the pressure of this problem. How clever! He wiped his forehead as he realized that this was a close call . . . Whew!

36

Before we send Pilate to a hot eternity, let's consider what we might have done if we were consistent with our own past record. How often have we "passed the buck" to avoid blame for a mistake or to get around the responsibility of making an unpopular decision? How often have we looked for some way to get out of the responsibility so it wouldn't be charged to our account? How often has someone else had to take the blame of our wrong or indecision? Is there any of Pilate's "pass the buck" trait in us?

It takes a man, a genuine man, to say "I did it" when he goofs. It takes a man of courage to make a decision that would be unpopular with the crowd. But God is always looking for such living, earth-walking specimens. Of course, you realize that some day soon you'll be called to give full account for your deeds. You'll not be able to point to the heavenly ledger and say the recording angel made a mistake. You won't be able to pass the buck then!

But why leave it to eternity to reveal your manliness — or lack of it? Next time you're tempted to pass the buck, pass it — from your left hand into your right one! Saying "I'm responsible" marks a man as a man. Are you one?

PRAYER: In my pride I've "passed the buck" to make others think more highly of me than I am entitled. As I accept the responsibility for all my deeds, even my misdeeds, let me seek only Your approval, Your forgiveness, and the clear record in heaven. Amen.

SCRIPTURE: They were full of sorrow, and began
to say, one after another, Lord, Is it I? . . . Then
Judas, he who was betraying him, said openly, Master
is it I? Jesus answered, Thy own lips have said it.
— *Matthew 26:22, 25, Knox*

16 When a Man Asks, "Lord, Is It I?"

Some men know they've committed wrong deeds, yet when an accusing finger is pointed toward them, they have the audacity to ask, "Who, me?" Judas was one of this kind of men.

Up to the point of our text, Judas had succeeded in covering his betraying intentions and deeds. He had given the impression of being as committed to Christ as were the other disciples. The other disciples didn't expect that he would get involved in such an act. Wasn't he the trusted treasurer of the group? They had committed their money to his accounting, to his trustworthiness. Now he's pointed out as the betrayer of their leader. Surely it can't be!

Betraying deeds are not usually done in the open. They are unknown until the last, too-late hour. Quite often such deeds seem inspired by a loss of faith in the leader. To break an association with such a leader, especially with an outstanding person, one becomes the easy prey of the temptation to become rash in either words or actions. Judas submitted to this temptation.

As far as we know, Judas was a normal man with normal desires and performing normal good deeds. At least this seemed true up to the point of betrayal. He guarded the apostolic treasury with great diligence. Once he even felt it was necessary to rebuke Christ for accepting the pouring of expensive ointment on His feet when the proceeds of a sale could at least have helped many of the poor people around Him. Furthermore, upon examining Judas' record, we don't find any previous rebellion. So the argument from silence could only prove Judas as an ordinary man, an accepted good fellow among the twelve.

What caused the sudden twist of character? What led him to betray Christ for the short-changed amount of thirty pieces of silver? Could it have been his good trait gone sour?

Aren't most of us only a step or two away from betrayal? The other disciples all thought they might be guilty. With sorrowful lamentations they cried. "Lord, is it I?" These weren't men who never had dirty hands. They were a rough lot — fishermen, a tax gatherer, etc. They were men. And the greater evidence of their manliness was their soul-searching ability and analysis, "Yes, Lord, possibly it is I!" They knew that within lurked the ugly possibility of betraying Jesus Christ.

What kept the eleven from betraying their Master? Can we fully blame Judas' act upon predestination — he had no other choice? Let us rather admit that Judas had a soul for which he was morally responsible. But in condemning him for his act, let us check our own moral responsibility. We haven't taken any final steps to betray Christ. But each of us must admit that his number lies somewhere between one and eleven. "Lord, is it I?"

PRAYER: Betrayed Saviour, let the blood of Your cross cover the betrayal that lurks in my soul — the betrayal that so easily comes to the surface and enthrones self by dethroning You. Keep my soul sensitive toward You lest I hear Your condemning words, "Thou hast said." Amen.

SCRIPTURE: Hear, O our God; for we are despised: and turn back their reproach upon their own head . . . So we built the wall; and all the wall was joined together unto half the height thereof: for the people had a mind to work. — *Nehemiah 4:4, 6, ASV*

17 Will a Sneer Stop a Saint?

Wall-builder Nehemiah had many reasons for quitting his job. Chief among them was the sneering techniques of two neighboring kings, Sanballet and Tobiah. Nehemiah had many reasons to go home to his wife and say, "I can't take it any longer. I'm quitting. They can get someone else to do the leading on this project."

Mockery squelches many good endeavors. It's one of the mean weapons in Satan's arsenal. Sanballet first demonstrated with a temper tantrum (Nehemiah 4:1), but this had less effect upon the Jews than his mocking words. Notice the tantrum was followed by his mockery of the Jews.

Satan loves to sneer! He knows that this method proves victorious even among the most manly of us. If we dare say it, we could see why mockery might affect the weaker sex. But how can we explain it among men? How strong are we when we allow a sneer to stop not only our saintliness but also the work we are willing to do as saints?

What do you do when men sneer or mock your Christian commitment or testimony? Many pull the mud-turtle act until the tormentors leave. Some pull the hare act and disappear in fright. Have you ever done either of these when someone has made fun of your Christian life? Are you a man at such times?

40

What did Nehemiah do? "Hear, O our God: for we are despised." He was man enough to admit that mockery was effective as a tool to thwart a project. A power greater than personal cleverness was needed to produce victorious results along the wall. Only God could help. So Nehemiah did what some men think is sissyish — he prayed. And God answered!

"So we built the wall." Prayer didn't stand alone. He didn't simply call a prayer meeting and expect God to eliminate the problem of the mockers. He insisted that feet and hands keep pace with their hearts. The victory came through a combination of worship and words and work. The fact that the people had "a mind to work" led to the victory.

How long have you been praying that God will knock over your tormentors or opposition? This is far too common in our evangelical churches. We don't seem to be men enough to recognize that work and worship cannot be separated in Christian experience. In fact, some have so mixed up their doctrine of works that they are afraid to do any good for fear some critical brethren might charge them of working for their salvation.

Let the enemy sneer. You have work to do and no one can stop you if God is on your side. The enemy's sneers cannot stop the saint. But the saint must keep the trowel of Christian endeavor busy and the mortar of Christian work moist. A sneer can't stop a saint if he's intent on finishing the work God has given him to do.

PRAYER: Manly Saviour, save me from hiding or running away from the people that would sneer at my efforts for Christ. Give me energy to keep busy doing Your work. Give me grace to keep calling on You for a refreshing supply of life. I want to build Your Kingdom. Amen.

SCRIPTURE: And the women sang one to another as they played, and said,

Saul hath slain his thousands,
And David his ten thousands.

— *I Samuel 19:7, ASV*

18 When Others Get the Credit

Some men, like David, deserve the credit they receive from the cheering crowds. They have performed well against many odds. This pleases onlookers. So it was with David on his return from the battle between the Israelites and the Philistines. At the same time, King Saul returned from the battle. But David outdid Saul in the battling. Therefore the public acclaim went to the younger man. The women lauded the feats of the ruddy young battler. While doing so, they discredited the victory of Saul over the enemy.

It is entirely possible for us to get into a similar situation, not on the battlefield or in numbering thousands of dead enemy soldiers, but in hearing the praises going to others. The way we react when someone else gets the praise demonstrates what kind of men we are.

How did Saul, the King of Israel, react when David received the praise? Did he add his personal congratulations? Hardly. "And Saul was very wroth, and the saying displeased him . . . and Saul eyed David from that day and forward" (I Samuel 18:8, 9). The eye of jealousy turned into an eye of hate. Soon Saul was seeking ways to kill the newly acclaimed hero. His hate-inspired pursuits of young David make adventurous reading in Sunday School junior departments around the world, but they hardly make it into the annals of a great man.

Maintaining a graceful attitude when someone else gets praise beyond that given to you is the mark of a mature Christian man. To allow another to be lauded in your presence, without displaying or harboring jealousy, shows mature character. And to allow someone to be praised for something that should be attributed to you is a mark of greatness. Few of us attain to this level of personality development. Most men see to it, even subtly or even while proclaiming "I don't want any credit for it" that credit gets to the *right* party.

Even Christians must be on the alert to check the jealousy that creeps into almost any life unawares when facing situations similar to the David-Saul encounters. Jealousy easily ferments into hatred. John wrote, "Whosoever hateth his brother is a murderer" (I John 3:15). You don't need a magnifying glass to see this fermenting process in today's world. It's everywhere.

When other men get the credit, what do you do? Are you man enough to join those who give the praise by letting credit come where it is due? Or do you sulk by yourself with green eyes? The Lord has both an earthly and a heavenly blessing for the man who can slap the other fellow on the back when he should be praised himself. Sulk or smile when others get the credit, it's up to you.

PRAYER: Lord, there's too much jealousy in the world for me to add to it. Forgive me for ever being a credit-grabber when I should be praising others. Help me to sincerely appreciate the accomplishments of those around me. Amen.

19 *Pride Hinders Progress*

If pride was prerequisite to greatness, then all men should take at least one lesson from Naaman. The great captain of Syria's hosts made a pompous presentation to Israel's king and then to the prophet Elisha. "Look who I am. Elisha, I'm here! Come out and bow."

All the outward demonstration of self-importance paraded itself to cover up a great need. Naaman was physically bankrupt. Proud to the hilt . . . "but he was a leper" (II Kings 5:1). Balloon chestedness couldn't cover the fact of his spotted skin. All the pomp of his parading before the prophet's home wouldn't remove the ugly open pock marks of his leprosy.

Naaman's pride was a transparent sham to the motive-piercing powers of the prophet. Elisha didn't even push back his tent flap to see the dignitary's haughty prancing. He quietly sent a servant to inform Naaman of the God-appointed remedy.

On hearing the remedy, "Go and wash in Jordan seven times, and thy flesh shall come again to thee, and thou shalt be clean" (II Kings 5:10), the mighty man of valor huffed and puffed. He even blew off a little steam! Hmmph! He was insulted. But take it or leave it, it was his own pride that stood in the way of his cleansing. Couldn't the prophet at least recognize him? And to think of it — dip seven times in the muddy Jordan River.

Pride usually devises schemes of its own to save face. Naaman was no exception. "Are not Abana and Pharpar, rivers of Damascus, better than all the waters of Israel? May I not wash in them and be clean?" he asks. But as long as his pride asserted itself, his cleansing did not come.

Be honest with yourself, have there ever been times when your pride hindered the progress of your spiritual life? your home life? your business advancement? even your healing? Some men are even too proud to seek the help of a physician when they need it. They'd rather resort to home remedies similar to the scheme of Naaman than to admit they needed the help that only others could give.

When Naaman's chest deflated and he realized all his schemes would fail, he discovered that humility produced the greatest results. The prophet's scheme brought cleansing. So he dipped according to the prophetic formula and came up clean. You'd expect nothing else!

To hurdle pride takes every ounce of manliness a man can muster. But when the hurdle is leaped, great strides can be made in a man's relationship to God, himself, and others. Does the pride of thinking you a mature, strong, self-sufficient man hinder your progress? "Go wash seven times. . . ."

PRAYER: Creator God, You have every right to show pride, yet we read that Christ humbled himself and became a no-reputation man. Bring me to the place where I am His follower not only in doctrine but in practical living. Amen.

SCRIPTURE: When Samuel asked Jesse, "Are these all your sons?" he replied, "There is still the youngest; you see, he is tending the sheep." Samuel said to Jesse, "Send and get him, for we shall not sit down until he is here."

— *I Samuel 16:11, Berkeley*

20 Do You Have Any More Sons?

Why God chooses one man for special service and passes another by is a question that only He can answer, if He ever will. David's being selected as king would surprise the politically oriented persons of today's world. In our terms, "he just didn't have it. He wasn't a politician in any sense of the word."

Look at David's qualifications: the youngest, keeper of sheep, ruddy cheeked and withall of a beautiful (some say fair) countenance, good to look at. But good looks and outdoor complexion are hardly prerequisites for becoming top ruler of a nation. But these were all included in God's choice of David as successor to Saul.

Seven of Jesse's sons paraded before Samuel. But God kept saying no. Then Samuel asked, "Do you have any more sons?"

Perchance the reader is a father. Who from among your children would you offer as a potential top-flight leader of your country? Do you have a son or daughter whom you think "just doesn't have it?"

Let's see why God passed up the first seven sons. After Samuel viewed one son of Jesse "the Lord said unto Samuel,

Look not on his countenance, or on the height of his stature
. . . for the Lord seeth not as man seeth; for man looketh on
the outward appearance, but the Lord looketh on the heart"
(I Samuel 16:7). The criteria of God penetrate beyond outward evaluations and observations.

Possibly God is calling your "just-doesn't-have-it" son into
some full-time ministry. Possibly that son will fit into a pas-
torate or some missionary endeavor. Remember, God looks on
the heart. He sees inner motives. He sees the potential man
in the boy. He knows what the boy can become. He holds
the blueprint of that child's destiny.

You ought to praise God for any discernment a servant of
the Lord, another Samuel, who knows God intimately enough
to discern whom the Lord is calling. Work with that Samuel
in bringing your child into a full realization of God's claims
upon your child's life.

And as you view the children of others, especially if you
are in a Sunday School teaching situation, be wise in your
discernment of their potentials. Some, who today are class
cutups, can develop into the spiritual and moral giants of a
few years hence. If you can obtain some of the discerning
power of Samuel in this matter, you are a valuable prophet
in God's present Kingdom. You'll be able to ask, Do you
have any more sons? God wants even the one playing in the
alley!

PRAYER: All-wise God, I don't fully understand Your
choice of servants. Let me not hinder even one from
surrendering his life to You. Here Lord, I yield my son
to Your guiding influence. Help me to be sensitive to
Your calling to my children no matter how talented
or untalented they might be this day. Amen.

SCRIPTURE: So they hanged Haman on the gallows that he had prepared for Mordecai.

— *Esther 7:10, ASV*

21 *Scheming to Self-Ruin*

Political assassinations dot history like polka dots on grandma's apron. One quickly remembers the shocking news of the assassination of John F. Kennedy. Unfortunately, murder plots so often succeed even when appropriate security has been made. But Haman's method wasn't so blunt. He schemed in the open. Everyone knew what he planned. Sad but true, his plot to rid himself of the opposition almost worked. He had succeeded in building the gallows and the scaffold necessary for the hanging of Mordecai. Suddenly the plot backfired as King Ahasuerus recognized Mordecai's contributions to the kingdom and Esther uncovered Haman's scheme.

Haman's way of gaining the prominent position becomes as dangerous as walking between land mines on a battlefield. The very items he placed to eliminate the opposition became the instruments of his personal downfall. He schemed himself to ruin.

Let's backtrack a little. Was it necessary for Haman to lay such careful plans to ruin Mordecai? If Haman must fulfill the hatred of his heart for the Jews — Yes. If he found no alternative than the destruction of any political occupant of his place of prominence — Yes. But if he could see Mordecai as a fellow laborer for a good purpose — No.

48

If he could see the greater gains of the kingdom being accomplished through various talented men — No.

Let's not "Shame, Shame" Haman until we check our personal records. How do we deal with opposition — even in the church? Occasionally Hamanism even raises its ugly head and gets recorded in church proceedings. Some seem bent on being on top of the pile — leaders by pressure. Any trick to get to the top seems to be approved in their minds. But sometime these tricks backfire. Thus the church is saved of many dictatorial leaders. God has a way of setting up those who rightfully belong on top.

Hamanism might be a temptation in this world of aggressive competition. The clever and the ambitious seem to be constant winners. In many cases they seem to do it by Haman's methods. But before God, all such scheming will lead to self-ruin. He who would destroy others must himself be destroyed.

If you are faced with opposition that seems to be creeping into your position of importance, beware — Hamanism lurks in the unconscious parts of your soul, ready to be put to use. To overcome the temptation to suppress others, recognize that you have been called by God to fulfill certain tasks. Others also have been called. The Lord has a place for you even if someone must take your position or get the prominent position you'd like to occupy. Are you as manly as Mordecai to wait your turn at greatness, or will you use Haman's approach and eventually end in self-ruin?

PRAYER: Lord, save me from being full of schemes when I seem overshadowed by others of importance. Implant a satisfaction in my soul that allows others to be great even when I am unnoticed. Amen.

SCRIPTURE: But Jonah rose up to flee unto Tarshish from the presence of the Lord — *Jonah 1:3, Berkeley*

22 *When a Man Runs from God*

The historical account of Jonah's experience is more than a whale of a story. It's the prototype of many Christian lives. And before you fish for an excuse, ask yourself, "Have I obeyed God every time He has called me?" The Jonah trick surely isn't a claim to mature manhood; that we'd all admit.

Jonah's task was this: go to the great city of Nineveh "and cry against it; for their wickedness is come up before me" (Jonah 1:2). Today's equivalent: go to the great city of Chicago or Detroit — one lonely person against millions — and tell them they are sinners facing almost immediate doom! How would you like that assignment? Yet this is what God told Jonah to do.

The easy way out: run away from God. Go in the opposite direction. Jonah thought he could do this successfully. That's where the fish story comes in, you know! It's not the invention of an unlucky fisherman. Jonah knew it by personal experience. God had it preserved and recorded for your benefit.

You can always find an alternate to what God wants you to do. You can even find a good thing to supplant the exact directions given by God. There's always some good that you can do. The Creator has endowed every man with the powers of reason to figure out the course of his life. It doesn't take much ingenuity to invent a way to escape the exact will of God.

Jonah found a ship headed toward Joppa. As a paying passenger he probably had the right to make himself comfortable. "But the Lord . . ." (Jonah 1:4). These words demand watching. Ah yes, Jonah had a comfortable alternate plan, but the Lord had determined that Jonah was His prophet for Nineveh. No one else would do at that time. So God got Jonah to Nineveh by His method!

Maybe God hasn't sent a violent storm to upset your small rowboat; nor has He sent a big fish to teach you a lesson. Nevertheless, He has His method of proving that you can't run from Him when your course has had heaven's blueprinting. Momentarily, He might allow you to go on your merry way, but sooner than you might think, He changes your course. Beware, a possible violent change of direction lurks around the next curve.

Possibly an experience of running away from God taught the Psalmist the impossibility of accomplishing such an endeavor. He wrote these solemn words" "Whither shall I go from thy spirit? or whither shall I flee from thy presence? If I ascend up into heaven, thou art there: if I make my bed in hell, behold, thou art there" (Psalm 139:7, 8).

He who would run from God usually has a whale of a story to tell when he returns!

PRAYER: How often, O Lord, have I heard You speak to me, saying, "Arise, go," and I have stood still or have fled from Your will. Give this cowardly heart of mine the vigor that willingly accomplishes the things to which I am sent. And help me to say yes the first time you speak to me. In the name of Him who told the Father, "Not my will, but Thine." Amen.

SCRIPTURE: Meanwhile the Lord had appointed a
great fish to swallow Jonah, and Jonah was in the belly
of the fish three days and three nights.

— *Jonah 1:17, Berkeley*

23 *Tell Me That Fish Story Again*

Scofield notes, "No miracle of Scripture has called forth
so much unbelief." Why is this so?

One could easily imagine the skepticism which greeted Jonah
on the beach as he journeyed toward Nineveh and told the
dramatic story of his being swallowed by a big fish. "Just
how big did you say that fish was?" they probably asked as
they compared the fish he talked about to those that were
caught in previous fishing expeditions. Actually, Jonah didn't
get a full view of the monster. He could only give some
description of the inner walls of the fish's stomach. He didn't
carry a camera to get a shot just as he hit water or just when
he hit land three days later. And it doesn't take much stretch-
ing of the imagination to hear the children of Nineveh asking
him to tell the big fish story in every speech he gave.

Can't you hear Jonah's answers to their questions and their
reactions to his statements, not about the fish, but about his
activities inside the slimy fish. "I prayed in the fish's belly.
'I cried by reason of my affliction unto the Lord' [Jonah 2:2].
This is all that matters to me as far as the big fish is concerned."

How do you answer men when they question the big fish
story? Jonah and the big fish dominate the questionings of
outsiders. They've heard about this fish story and want to
hear your revised and standard versions.

You can't explain a miracle. All you can do is retell it.
God's workings are beyond natural explanation. He often
uses natural means — in this case a big fish — to accomplish

His desired purposes. The manner of His operation can only be classified as supernatural — a miracle. You can tell the fish story, but the explanation remains one of God's secrets.

The main thrust of the story centers not in the length or the weight or the color or the kind of fish that swallowed the hookless bait. The central truth comes in determining why the fish swallowed Jonah, clothes and all. If you tell the story, be sure to state how God intended to fulfill His purposes through the life of Jonah and how Jonah seemed to make it a little difficult for God to get the work going. Tell the futility of running from God. Tell how God preserved Jonah to accomplish the purpose for which he was called.

Have you ever told this fish story to the fellow who stares at you when you are shaving? Yes, he needs to hear it again. In case he has become skeptical about miracles — re-tell this whale of a story. In case he has become careless about obeying the Lord's commands to get up and get going — then tell him what happened to Jonah. In case he has become calloused about the needs of so many others — tell him of Jonah's eagerness to preach after the fishy ordeal.

In case no one ever brings this story to your attention, it's a good one to use as an opener to talk about the Lord's will in your life and for theirs. Most men have had some fisherman's luck. Take pride in this big fish story. You can use this top-notch fish story to lead them to a knowledge of God's working in and for their lives. Use the telling of this story to point others to the Creator. Be sure to tell that fish story again.

PRAYER: Sharpen my faith in Your ways of working. Since You are supernatural, help me to expect You to act consistent with Your nature. Help me to accept all miracles You perform. And in explaining them, give me grace to confess my limited understanding of Your methods. I accept You as the best proof of Your acts. Amen.

SCRIPTURE: So when God saw what they did, how they turned from their evil way, God relented of the punishment which He had said He would inflict on them, and He did not do it. But this greatly displeased Jonah, and he grew angry. — *Jonah 3:10; 4:1, Berkeley*

24 A Whole City Was Saved, So What?

Scared stiff after the episode in the fish's belly, Jonah rushed to Nineveh with God's message of doom. The Ninevites repented. The entire city was saved from impending destruction. You'd think Jonah would build a temple in which all Ninevites could join him in praise to God for His mercy. Did he not exclaim, "I know that Thou art a gracious God, and merciful, slow to anger, and of great kindness . . ." (Jonah 4:2). Yet, after the whole city was saved, he possessed a "so what" attitude. He even wanted to die after his exhausting preaching mission came to a close.

Can it be possible, that, in dealing with sinful men, a man becomes so calloused that even the salvation of sinners hardly dents his heart? Could the presentation of the message of God's mercy become so mechanical, that, when men actually accept it, the proclaimer fails to recognize the transformation in men's souls? Could it be that a man becomes so concerned with his personal accommodations that he really isn't concerned about the desperate condition of others? Has religion become just another business transaction? Jonah's preaching and testimony vibrated with words of warning, but his heart was far removed from his words. He possessed an "I don't care" attitude.

Jonah could have become afflicted with the type of twentieth-century lack of concern for individuals. He could have been enraptured by the responses of the hundreds, yet untouched by the single repenting sinners. In fact, they could have been a bother to him. Modern day evangelism often promotes group response. This can cause the evangelist to become a religious professional.

Even though Nineveh bowed in sackcloth and ashes, Jonah's loss of compassion compelled him to believe that God's judgment should still be their portion. "Sure they were saved, but they really deserve. . . ."

The calculating mind must be held in constant check. You can't simply number those who have been transformed by the power of Christ. They are more than religious statistics. They demand compassionate concern. Rejoice that God has spared each individual from the terrible torments of a hot eternity. Become akin to those in heaven who rejoice whenever one sinner repents (Luke 15:7).

If Jonah would have kept his concern at the high pitch of compassion after the Ninevites repented, he wouldn't have moaned about his personal state of affairs. Beware lest you also succumb to the temptation of self-interest fed by self-pity. The Lord needs you to continue in compassion as a teacher of those who have just recently found The Way. Even if a multitude were to flock to the revival altar, remember that each is an individual — some so young they can't even tell their right hand from their left (Jonah 4:11).

PRAYER: O compassionate Christ, keep my heart tender as Yours so I may lead new converts into deeper truths. Help me to see beyond myself, beyond the masses to each person. In the mighty name of Him who wept over the city of Jerusalem but didn't forget even the least individual in need. Amen.

SCRIPTURE: Simon Peter said to them, I am going fishing. They said to him, we are going with you too. They went out and got into a boat, but that night they caught nothing. — *John 21:3, Williams*

25 When It's Frivolous to Go Fishing

Fishing attracts robust men who make it their trade. It attracts many others who make it their hobby. We do not know if Peter led the other disciples back into his livelihood or rather for an evening of relaxation. Possibly it was only a means of relaxation — a time to rethink everything that had gone on in Jerusalem.

The situation in Jerusalem hadn't been relaxing. Jesus had been betrayed by Judas for thirty pieces of silver. Peter had denied his Lord three times before the cock crowed twice. None of the disciples could do anything to prevent Christ from being crucified by an angry rioting mob. Three days later, Peter along with the other disciples received the news that Jesus had risen as He predicted. Peter conducted his own investigation of the empty tomb. Jesus appeared to the disciples on several occasions. Through three years of teaching, Jesus had prepared the twelve to carry the message unto all men. Surely Peter must have been aware of the responsibilities that the Lord had placed upon them. So this call to the boats and nets seems a little out of order. At such an hour, it's frivolous to go fishing.

Why is it that men so often shift from the sublime to the superficial? What causes men to propose a fishing trip a few minutes after being carried to spiritual mountain peaks by a pastor's sermon? What causes men to propose and practice frivolous activities when stupendous things have just taken place?

Isn't Peter simply our prototype? He had yet to catch the

vision of what God would do with a totally surrendered man. He still controlled the reigns of his personal life. And accompanying this self-interest was Peter's impetuous desire to keep life sparkling. He could always be counted upon to create new ideas, to inaugurate a new program. Right or wrong, when an idea popped into his head, he expressed it. On several occasions this led to his downfall. "Let's go fishing" at a time when they should have been shouting resurrection news throughout the city!

If we would keep our activities to ourselves, we wouldn't be such a drag on the church's program. But men, we all love company. We want a partner in sport. What would happen if we were spiritually mature to know when we should go fishing, go bowling, go skating? Are we mature enough to know when we shouldn't even whisper the name of these enjoyable activities?

The Lord is not opposed to recreation. But it thwarts His program when it dominates our thinking. It thwarts His when we are among those who absent themselves from volunteering to carry His message to the ends of the earth, or even into our neighborhood. At times when we should be proclaiming we are often somewhere playing.

Notice, the Lord didn't rebuke Peter for fishing. He blessed him in it. But notice also, Peter never went fishing again. Somehow his sense of values was completely changed. He found that at certain times even fishing is a frivolous use of time.

PRAYER: Lord, I realize there's nothing morally wrong with recreation unless it interferes with more important activities. Give the discernment that I need to use my time properly lest I indulge in frivolous activities that have no meaning. Help me to remember that You spent Your life on earth always considering the value of working in the moments of time that were Yours. Amen.

SCRIPTURE: So Eli said to Samuel, "Go, lie down again, and when He calls you, say, "Speak, Lord, for thy servant is listening." — *I Samuel 3:9, Berkeley*

26 Distinguishing God's Call to a Boy

Unfortunately this text does not state the spiritual obtuseness of Eli. All of us well remember how the boy Samuel heard the Lord calling and how Eli replied, "Sh-h-h — I called not; lie down again" (I Samuel 3:5). Eli couldn't distinguish the voice of the Lord calling to the boy.

Face it, man, could you distinguish when God was calling your son? Did you help him respond immediately to God's call?

Eli was in the religion business. It was his life — he was a priest. He knew the sacred Scriptures. He knew from study and experience how God called to men in special circumstances and to special service. And in his day, as throughout much of the Old Testament, we have evidence of God audibly speaking to men. If it was so difficult for a life-time worker in the priesthood to distinguish God's call to Samuel, is it not justifiable for us to be slow along these lines — slow even to the extent of being excused?

Eli wasn't excused for his slowness of heart. In chapter 2, God warned Eli of his sinfulness. It was this sinfulness that dulled his spiritual perception. Sin dulled his soul, making him hard of hearing.

Praise God, the Lord eventually got through to Eli. That glorious dawning upon his soul brought him to realize that the Lord was speaking to the boy. Then come the words of our text. He knew how to direct the boy to the Lord.

Can you praise God that He has invaded your life with a consciousness of His will? Are you so submitted to God that you'll be able to distinguish the will of God for the younger generation? It takes considerable submission to God to become aware of the needs of the generation we seek to help.

Really, can you point someone to Jesus Christ in a way that that person will respond in faith to Him? Have you ever tried to explain the way of salvation to a boy? Have you succeeded in leading that boy to personal faith and response toward the Saviour?

The Lord's call to youth re-echoes His call to adults. It's a call to service and surrender. Eli told Samuel to answer, "Speak, Lord, for thy *servant* heareth." The attitude developed in Samuel's heart by the older man was that men are servants of God. Samuel's call meant Samuel's service.

What confidence Samuel possessed. Eli, the man, told him how to answer God! The mighty arm of the world-worn priest rested on the not-yet-developed shoulder muscles of Samuel. The whisper of godly instruction. Now the boy could face God by himself.

The Lord came to that boy. With confidence he uttered the words taught by Eli. The Lord then instructed the boy in his life's labors.

Have you had the joy of Eli? Surely you've had the opportunity. What boy has answered God with the words, "Speak, Lord, for thy servant heareth," because of your witness?

PRAYER: Lord, make me sharp enough to recognize Your will first for myself and then for the boys near and dear to me. May they rise up to follow You at my suggestion. For Christ's sake. Amen.

27 Making Sure God Called You

You can't dictate God's will for me or for anyone else! Nor can you dictate the method whereby others gain assurance of God's will. We've trusted the clichés too long — Pray about it. Read the Bible, etc. For some people, nothing short of fleece-laying will settle the issue!

Being able to say about one's life and actions, "I'm doing the will of God," is no insignificant matter. Literally one is saying, "I, as a small man, am accomplishing the plan of the unlimited God." Such a statement would be blasphemous or presumptuous if it wasn't supported by serious consideration of all the facts involved. Determining God's will cannot be a casual happenstance.

Gideon's fleece has become the most famous sheepskin of history. He had heard God's claim upon his life. He offered a sacrifice in honor to the divine call. Yet, down in his soul he had a reservation. He wanted all doubt removed. Thus he tells God, "I will put fleece of wool in the floor, and if the dew be on the fleece only . . . then shall I know" (v. 37). This was not enough. He must reverse the order — dry fleece, dewed ground.

Call this *doubt* if you want to. Why not call it *determination?* Why not view it as *confirmation?* No man should rightfully leap into his life-changing situations until he senses the will of God in some manner, possibly only known within himself. Gideon was no doubter, and above all — no fool!

Probably God isn't calling you to be our country's battle leader. Maybe the greatest battle you'll ever fight has your soul as the battlefield. Maybe you'll never be pushed into a position of authority. But knowing God's will for your life in relationship to your task, and to your daily endeavor in that task, is as important to you and to God as the choice of Gideon.

Gideon's "let me prove, I pray thee," indicates an intimate contact with God. He knew the art of ordinary conversation with Divinity. His expression wasn't one of guesswork, but one of confidence in the character of God.

Interestingly, Gideon proved God's will right in the place of his employment. He didn't rush off to some high mountain. He didn't lock himself in some secluded monastery. He didn't form a week-end retreat. God's messenger spoke to him as he was threshing wheat by his winepress. He offered sacrifices there. Finally he put out the fleece "in the floor" — in the threshing floor.

As God speaks to you concerning His plan for the future of your life — do you have to retreat somewhere to think things over? Do you have the Gideon-type ability to think things through while remaining at your presently assigned work?

Have you taken the proper steps in determining that God has called you? that He has ordained you to perform the task you are now doing? By what method did you arrive at being able to say, "This is the will of God for me"? Or are you drifting your own way without having confidence that you are performing according to divine planning?

Gideon's fleece indicated the maturity of character that made him capable of the leadership position assigned to him. Are you man enough when it comes to knowing God's will?

PRAYER: Lord, guide me to be fully persuaded that I am living according to the Divine blueprint. I don't take this for granted. Rather, indicate to me through specific circumstances that my walk is right. I too, want the confirming witness of some type of dry fleece. Amen.

SCRIPTURE: And when they reached the water, the Lord's command to Gideon was, Separate those who lap the water like dogs, and those who go down on their knees to drink. There were only three hundred that took up water in their hands and lapped it . . . the Lord said to Gideon, these three hundred men who lapped the water shall win you deliverance.

— *Judges 7:5, 6, Knox*

28 Separating
the Men from the . . .

Selecting an army on the basis of how soldiers drink water would surely justify psychiatric examination of the general. Regardless of the era, such a method would seem not only ridiculous, but a tremendously risky approach. But God takes such risks!

Again we wonder at God's judgment in choosing those who serve His purposes. Wouldn't there be a better way to test men for warfare? Why not measure their biceps? Why not test their sprinting or boxing abilities? Why not put them through a rigorous course of calisthenics?

God's method in selecting Gideon's mighty three hundred seems ridiculous. But God knew what He was doing. He wanted men who were alert. He wanted men who didn't even have to change positions to fight the enemy. And three hundred such men compared favorably to several thousand of the kneel-and-sip variety. God separated the men from the. . . .

If God used similar methods for selecting workers in your church, among which group would you be placed — among the select group, the men among men, or among the general group He sent back to mature? The demands of the hour, compared to the demands placed upon Gideon's three hundred, necessitate men of the same calibre. Would God find any in your church capable of doing battle for Him? Would you be dressed in a soldier's uniform? If God separated the men from the . . . , where would you find yourself?

So much time is lost because of the necessity of juggling positions before we are able to serve. The time is lost because we aren't alert to opportunities. The service of the church demands instant men — men previously prepared through spiritual calisthenics, who are now alert volunteers. Then the enemy, who might be much stronger in number, will take a beating.

God not only selected the three hundred — separating the men from the . . . , but He empowered them to do battle. And once you are selected by God for His appointed task, be assured that He'll supply all the necessary armament so you can perform victoriously. The church is built by the three hundreds, not by the thousands who relax to enjoy themselves and gain all the benefits without caring to be alert to God's call.

God constantly separates the men from the. . . . Among which group are you? If it's not in the three hundred, take the necessary steps to learn how to sip without kneeling!

PRAYER: Lord, I confess my desire to live an easy Christian life, reaping where I have not sown, benefiting where I have not worked. Fill me with a desire to serve, to labor, to spend and be spent, not for reward, but in the knowledge that I am doing God's work. Keep me surprisingly alert so I can say yes at a moment's notice. Amen.

SCRIPTURE: But his father and mother replied to him, "Is there no woman at all among the girls of our own people or kinsmen, that you must seek a wife among the uncircumcised Philistines?" Samson answered his father, "Get her for me; for she pleases me well." — *Judges 14:3, Berkeley*

29 When Picking a Wife — Watch Out!

Love based upon infatuation isn't a twentieth-century weakness. Samson was likewise afflicted. All he could see was Delilah's physical form. She was sexy and knew how to appeal to Samson's sexual interests. Nothing else mattered. No one of his narrower religious clan back home had as much eye appeal or emotional stimulating powers.

How are the mighty fallen? Often by the charms of beautiful women. Women have trimmed many a great man down to his stature. Someone has facetiously exclaimed, "Woman caused man to sin in the first place, and she's continued her art ever since!"

"I'm a strong man. She'll never distract me from my religion. I'll win her to my way of thinking and believing." If you could have listened in on the discussion between Samson and his father, you'd probably have heard such words. He knew that Delilah's religion wouldn't mix with Judaism and that an unequal yoke doesn't work to the glory of God.

But Samson insisted, blinded by sensual desire, held in bondage by passion. Therefore his father, after a careful warning, allowed son Samson to pursue his marriage into heathendom.

Three thousand years haven't changed men every much. In most matters of love, logic is really not considered. Today's culture clamors for the satisfaction of a man's passions. And men just haven't developed emotionally to resist these clamorings. Samson would act the same today as he did then. Oh, how weak we really are!

What more could you expect of the Samson-Delilah mismatch? No more than what can be expected of any believer-nonbeliever mismatch today. The unequal yoke is always unequal. The cry of Samson's father was true, "Don't marry an enemy!"

Statistically, Samson had all the power to overcome any disadvantage such as marriage might produce. He had muscular superiority; he had religious heritage; he had Divine commissioning; he had wise parents. Every man likes to measure his strong assets. But Samson had weak emotions, gullible passions. Delilah therefore coupled her passionate love-making efforts to her political intrigue and brought her husband in line with those who controlled her life.

Possibly, if Samson were here today, he'd warn men that women catch men by circumventing their strong characteristics and by concentration on the weaker ones. He'd say, "When picking a wife — watch out!" For surely marriage should not be contracted with closed eyes in the presence of female charms. There's more to it than the satisfaction of one's sensual desires. Any marriage contracted on such passionate points will have many soul-rending conflicts until stability is established — if ever it can be.

PRAYER: Oh wise God, supply my soul with discernment in the delicate selection of a life mate. Help me to realize that genuine love comes from deep within the personality and finds the human form only secondary in importance. Amen.

30 What's the Secret of Your Strength?

Every man has some secrets by which he likes to measure his strength. Samson was no different, except his secrets were implanted in him by a covenant with God. In a foxy manner he thought that he could keep his secrets from the crafty, seducing Delilah.

Can you boast any secrets of strength? Samson was made strong by the above-mentioned covenant. "The child shall be a Nazarite to God from the womb to the day of his death" (Judges 13:7). Godly parents set him apart for a specific service through a holy dedication. The influence of this parent-God covenant cannot be underestimated.

In our era of rejection of parental instruction and guidance, it would be wise to consider the power of Samson. As long as he followed the vow made by his parents to God, he displayed unchallenged strength. As long as he fulfilled his obligations to God, he maintained mastery over any enemy — human or animal.

We trace Samson's strength directly to God. And ultimately any honest man must admit that God is the source of all strength — of body, mind, or soul. The very character of an individual is a gift from God. In Him and through Him and to Him are all things. Thus Paul could rightfully exclaim,

"I can do all things through Christ who strengtheneth me."

But Samson didn't tell Delilah his source of strength. He toyed with her mind like a father would play tricks on a child. In doing this, he also toyed with his parental covenant. He told Delilah to perform some strength tests. All proved futile. His secret was unknown. Unfortunately, through his weakness toward her passionate embraces, he later divulged his secret.

In a sense, every man should keep the secret of his inner strength locked deep in his soul — he should have a dynamic contact with God through a personal relationship with Jesus Christ. This will produce personal strength of character. And even though it can be vividly described to other men, yet it remains a personal secret because it is based upon a personal relationship with God — something that can only belong to the individual. This experience should be a man's prized possession. And once he possesses it, he can draw upon the resources of heaven for strength.

Of course, in a sense this becomes a secret, but it must be a secret each convert shares with the world. When others therefore respond to the Gospel, they too shall know the secret.

What is the secret of your strength? Does it lie in yourself or in your God? If Samson would only have depended upon the Secret of Eternal Strength, we'd have a far different story to tell to our children.

PRAYER: My strength comes from You, O Lord. Help me to make this more than a doctrinal truth. Let it be a dispositional reality. Then shall I be able to do all things through Christ. In His mighty name. Amen.

SCRIPTURE: At last he told her the truth. I am a Nazarite, he said; that is to say, I am consecrated to God from birth, and this hair of mine has never felt the touch of steel. If my hair were cut, my strength would leave me; I should lose it all, and become like other men. — *Judges 16:17, Knox*

31 Like Any Other Man

A narrow margin separates the strong from the weak, the popular from the unknown, the galant from the cowardly, the spiritual from the carnal.

Throughout his life, Samson lived in that narrow margin. It took only one vexing step to cross over from strength to weakness. The pity of Samson's plight was the way in which this transition took place — while he slept! That awful step brought blindness and imprisonment. One moment mastery — the next moment slavery!

Once Delilah learned the secret of his strength, she mastered the secret of his weakness. The parent-God covenant was broken and Samson "became weak . . . like any other man."

The margin separating any Christian from other men can be placed in the same category as the margin in Samson's life. The marginal area is a man's dedication to God. As long as a man stays within this marginal area, he's on the victory side. When he strays away from his dedication to God, he immediately opens himself up to defeat, weakness, carnality. He becomes like any other man.

The Christian is like other men, except for this marginal distinction of the presence of God in his life. As the Holy Spirit controls his personality, the Christian demonstrates a life above the lives of men around him. Once he enthrones himself, he becomes "weak like any other man."

The steps Samson took from galantry to slavery were very distinct. We have the whole story recorded in the book of Judges. The steps we take from dynamic Christian living to that of being like other men aren't always so easily delineated. Therefore we must guard our steps; we must submit them to the Lord; we must walk according to the Scripturally designated paths.

None of us wants to be like any other man. We all strive to be different. We all strive for mastery. We all aim at being head and shoulders above our peers. Only by submitting to God shall this truly be accomplished. A God-dominated life will always stand out among men. Carefully guard your steps lest you take a Samson-type downward journey from constant, victorious living to being like weak, sin-controlled men.

Perhaps you've already hit bottom; perchance you are grinding out days and years as the victim of defeat — there is hope. In prison, the sign of Samson's dedication and strength began to reappear. His strength started to leap in his body.

Through Jesus Christ, the mercy of God can restore you, And though you might carry the marks of your fall throughout the remainder of your life, much like Samson carried these marks in eyeless eye sockets, you can be forgiven, restored, cleansed. Once this happens to you, give all diligence to maintain a margin of spiritual victory in Christ.

PRAYER: I realize, O mighty God, that I could easily be weak like other men if it weren't for divine strengthening. Surround me with Your protective power lest I also slip. Through the empowering Christ, help me to maintain a margin in life that keeps me on Your side. Amen.

SCRIPTURE: However, if it seems wrong in your eyes to serve the Lord, choose today whom you will serve . . . Nevertheless, I and my house, we shall serve the Lord. — *Joshua 24:15, Berkeley*

32 *As for Me and My House*

When a man can include his kin in his vows, you've met a strong-charactered individual. No wonder God chose Joshua to conquer the Promised Land. When the conquest was nearing its end, also toward the end of the life of conqueror Joshua, he still could express his authority over his household. Israel had digressed from full allegiance to Jehovah. Many on the land were openly worshiping Canaanite gods and goddesses. Seemingly, true worship waned. Children had neglected the religion of their parents. Possibly parents had grown weary in their family religious instructions. But the faith of Joshua was firm and aggressive.

Joshua wasn't going to force his religion on other men. He had convictions that were personal, but he realized that no man's heart can be changed by force. Religious worship must come spontaneously through a person's love and devotion to God. Joshua knew that even though one's body might be forced into a worshiping position, that man's heart might be standing erect in refusal to pay homage to God. Therefore Joshua told Israel, "Choose you this day whom ye will serve."

But consider the strength of his religious beliefs and influence among his relatives. "As for me" is exceptionally clear. A man can speak for himself. Any manly fellow ought to be able to stand up and express himself with conviction. You are less than a true man if you are afraid to say, "As for me."

Joshua adds "and my house." He speaks for his relatives with the same authority that he speaks for himself. He made no apologies for doing thus. He knew them so well, he was absolutely convinced that he could and should speak for them. They probably had given him adequate assurance that they believed the same as he. As leader of his household, he influenced his relatives to believe and follow his God. This is a great compliment to the virility of his faith and leadership. Who of us can measure himself alongside this great man?

Lastly, notice that Joshua's kin decided against the downward trend of the nation. As for them, "we will serve the Lord," was their response to Joshua's leadership. They chose not to walk the easy road. Rather, they chose hardship as good soldiers of the Lord. He had led them down a circumspect road, a narrow path of righteousness. They seemed unashamed of Joshua's grandfatherly leadership or religion. To them, their religion was more virile than their aged leader. They seemed intent to keep it that way.

Man, who of us is capable of all this? Who of us is following in Joshua's footsteps? Who of us exerts this much influence among members of our families? Are we able to step from the "as for me" to the "as for me and my house" type of conviction and leadership in the religious affairs of those whom we love and cherish? Can we base the religion of our families on our personal convictions? Can we get them to practice our type of religion? Such a feat belongs to the man who intimately loves God and compassionately loves his kin. In this, God challenges men to accomplish what to ordinary men seems impossible.

PRAYER: God of Abraham, Isaac, Jacob, and Joshua, instill fresh courage in my soul so I can proclaim "as for me." Then let me love my kin into Your Kingdom in such a way that they too will follow You wholeheartedly. I long for the day when we shall serve the Lord. Make me dynamic in spirit so they'll choose to march according to Your orders. Amen.

SCRIPTURE: Now Peter was sitting outside in the courtyard, and a waiting-girl came up to him, and said, You, too, were with Jesus the Galilean. But he denied it before them all, and said, I do not understand what you mean. — *Matthew 26:69, 70, Williams*

33 Ashamed of Indentity

Why is it easier to deny than to defend one's faith in public? Does the inner personality mechanism have a weakness which more readily expresses itself in denial than in affirmation? Before we blame Peter for cowardice or any other personality flaw, let's take a good look at our own past performance. Have we ever been ashamed of Jesus Christ? Have we ever denied, either by audible expression or by silence, our connection with the Saviour? Have we always been loyal to our commitment to our God? Why this fear of being identified personally with our Creator-Redeemer? What's behind all this, anyway?

Let's be honest with ourselves. If we've turned our lives over to Jesus Christ, we've admitted our utter depravity; we've admitted our eternal weakness. It's a good thing. The man who can depend upon his own strength will never see his need of God. So obviously, when we're ashamed of our connection with Christ, it's simply our old nature dominating our lives and saying that we're not so bad in ourselves. Rather than being ashamed of Christ, we ought to be ashamed of ourselves. Somehow we need to learn how to express denial of self, not denial of the Saviour.

Satan succeeds in our lives by confusing the issue. He gets

us to deny our Lord when we should be denying our sinful lusts. It's the desire for self-affirmation, self-agrandizement, self-glory that makes us deny the Lord. The only sure cure is a daily reckoning of ourselves, as Paul says, to be dead indeed unto sin but alive unto God through Jesus Christ. Peter learned this at a later date.

At point blank range, we'd probably affirm our faith. But it's in the minute talk of life, in the ordinary pursuits of existing, that denial is more commonplace. Often we deny our Lord by saying nothing. We silently agree to some non-Christian concept or practice. We do not stand against sin or for the Lord. Lack of words or actions might be as great a denial as the calculated words of the impetuous New Testament fisherman.

Standing up for Jesus calls for a 168-hour per week life and lip testimony. It calls for taking the name of the Saviour with us in our homes, factories, offices, and places of amusement or recreation. It calls for a continuous conscious attempt to bring credit to the Master.

Denial is natural, too natural. Expression of belief takes courage. Only as we allow the Holy Spirit to take contol of our lives will we avoid the piercing wail of the crowing cock reminding us that we have slipped! He who would know the power over such denial must learn the secret of Romans 6:11.

PRAYER: Forgive me, Lord, for the multitude of times I've denied my identity with You. Help me to see that He who is in me is greater than any man, therefore I can be proud that I am identified with Him. Harmonize my life and lips in my attempts to proclaim my faith. Amen.

SCRIPTURE: Then Peter remembered Jesus' words, Before a cock crows, you will disown me three times. And he went outside and wept bitterly.

— *Matthew 26:75, Williams*

34 When a Man Cried

Men usually delegate tear shedding to the "weaker sex." Men only wipe their eyes in the wind or perchance at the time of some great emotional or spiritual crisis. It was at such an hour that Peter didn't care what other men thought of him — he wept bitterly.

Why is it that we think it's so manly to be dry-eyed. Why do we categorize crying as a sissy act? Why are we ashamed to be caught with red eyes? If crying demonstrates a good-to-have weakness, let's have our handkerchiefs available. If crying indicates that we, like Peter, realize our gross sin, let's weep out loud.

Previously, Peter pranced around the porch in utter self-confidence. He proudly disavowed any connection with the Man of Galilee. But he couldn't escape the soul-piercing words of Jesus even after he cursed at those who accused him of identity with the Master. Matthew tells us "Peter remembered." Memory of our sin-slanted souls ought to inspire tears of repentance.

Isaiah saw himself as he was in God's sight, and cried "Woe is me, for I am undone." Seeing ourselves in this light causes a spiritual crisis, a tear-shedding plea for forgiveness. When we see ourselves as we are, we can't help but weep.

74

On second thought, now that we've been saved through the death of Christ, shouldn't we be more sensitive about our Lord's reputation? Can we easily deny Him without feeling bitter disappointment within ourselves? Does Christ have so little meaning to our lives that we can deny Him one day and proclaim our allegiance the next day with few qualms of conscience?

Robust Peter had every right to cry. And so do we! Let's not seek to portray manliness upon false terms. When we should weep because of our sin or our timidity in witnessing to our identity with Christ, let's be the first to own up to our tears. A true man will have an occasionally dampened handkerchief. He will weep not only in his closet but whenever he realizes what pain he has produced in the heart of the Lord Jesus.

If more men would weep bitterly, we would know what the Scriptures mean when they describe Jesus as a Man of Sorrows. We would probably see more men turning to Him. We would see non-Christians realizing that Christians have both a passion toward God and a compassion toward men.

Peter had every right to go out and weep bitterly. Under similar circumstances only the hardhearted man would not cry. If weeping brings you into a fuller fellowship with Christ, cry, brother, cry!

PRAYER: Lord, make me sensitive about my sin and denial of identity with You that my eyes might become moistened with tears of repentance. Then in mercy, wipe the tears from my face. Help me to cry when I ought so to do. Amen.

35 *A Shirtsleeve Disciple*

Andrew's last name could easily have been "Mr. Do." No
matter where you read of him, he's active — he's accomplishing something on behalf of others. His Christ-related activity
all started after he heard John the Baptist preach — "One of
the two which heard John speak, and followed him, was
Andrew . . ." (John 1:40). As far as Andrew was concerned,
a follower expresses himself in activity. And again in John
12:22 we read of him, "Philip cometh and telleth Andrew;
and again Andrew and Philip tell Jesus."

One can readily picture Andrew with his shirtsleeves rolled
up past the elbows, ready to do something for someone. Service was a great motivating force within his personality. And
when he dedicated his life to Jesus Christ, this motivation was
at its highest and purest peak. It seems he delighted in relating
others to the Master without any regard for personal gain.
What could he get from a boy with only a sack lunch. What
could he get from a group of Greeks who wanted simply to
see Jesus? Surely his motives were clear in both of these
cases — he wanted to be of service to others.

Andrew lived a quiet but dramatic life. He probably didn't
think so — that's the way with people who are always getting
involved with helping others. Actually the reason his life

seems so dramatic is because ours are so lifeless. The man who is motivated to serve others will always live a dramatic life whether he realizes it or not. If more men in the church were like Andrew, it wouldn't look so unusual when a man rolls up his sleeves to do the Lord's work. Besides this, the world would soon realize that someone cares and that something dramatic is happening because of the many servant-saints.

Why is it that most men like to be spectators rather than participants? Why do we wait to see what someone else plans on doing before we pitch in and do the work? With so much to be accomplished in our times of crisis, the church has no need for those with the disease of spectatoritis. It has need for thousands of healthy, robust Andrews.

Andrew displayed marks of maturity — he knew that unless he rolled up his sleeves, possibly some people would never have an encounter with Christ. If he didn't bring them to Jesus, possibly no one would. Do you possess this maturity?

If you don't find some project to which you can give your talents and energies, then contact your pastor, your deacon or trustee board or your Sunday School superintendent. Then roll up your sleeves. The Lord wants volunteers for the Royal Order of Andrew.

PRAYER: Lord, I'm not afraid to get my hands dirty. Whatever task You have for me, I will do. Help me never to pass up an opportunity in which I can serve someone. I'd like to be known as a shirtsleeve follower of Yours. Amen.

36 When Facing Large Opposition

Today it is illegal to mismatch boxing opponents. A
lightweight is never matched with a heavyweight. But such
rules didn't apply for the David-Goliath match. The rules, set
by the Philistine giant, were: "Ho, Ho, Ho! Every Israelite
is afraid of me. I challenge any one of them to fight." How
embarrassed the giant must have been when he looked down
past his broad nose at his puny opponent. You can hear
his fellow soldiers taunt him with, "What a sissy you've turned
out to be, picking on this poor little boy."

All he could answer was, "He asked for it."

David refused the king's armor because he hadn't tried it.
He stayed with the tried-and-sure methods a shepherd boy
constantly used in shagging off wild animals. A few smooth
stones and a sling shot — that's all he needed.

Secondly, David committed himself and his cause to God and
trusted in divine energy. Such a committal could challenge the
shining armor of any giant. One small man with God on his
side reduces the stature of a Goliath considerably. In fact,
the size ratio was probably reversed.